QUEER
POWER!

PENGUIN WORKSHOP
An imprint of Penguin Random House LLC, New York

First published in the United Kingdom by HarperCollins,
an imprint of HarperCollins Publishers LLC, London, 2021

First published in the United States of America by Penguin Workshop,
an imprint of Penguin Random House LLC, New York, 2023

Copyright © 2021, 2023 by Dominic Evans

Visit us online at penguinrandomhouse.com.

Library of Congress Cataloging-in-Publication Data is available.

Manufactured in China

ISBN 9780593521359   10 9 8 7 6 5 4 3 2 1 TOPL

DOM & INK

QUEER

POWER!

ICONS, ACTIVISTS &

GAME CHANGERS

FROM ACROSS

THE RAINBOW

PENGUIN WORKSHOP

CONTENTS

LADY
PHYLL

INTRODUCTION 6

CHAPTER ONE 8
OUT, PROUD & VISIBLE

CHAPTER TWO 38
TRANS & NONBINARY POWER!

CHAPTER THREE 64
PROUD FAMILIES

CHAPTER FOUR 92
LOVE YOUR QUEER SELF!

CHAPTER FIVE 120
PRIDE POWER!

OUTRODUCTION 151
THANK YOU! 152
WAYS TO SUPPORT 153
HELPLINES 155
RESOURCES 156
SOURCES 160

INTRO

When I was growing up, I really struggled to see myself in many, if any, characters, anywhere. Where was my feminine homo, the lanky-legged queeroe of dreams that I could aspire to be? There were only so many years I could pretend to be Cheetara from *ThunderCats* or Ellie Sattler from *Jurassic Park* (Laura Dern, if you read this, I always look at a pink shirt and cream cargo-short combo and think of you fondly). And here's the thing: I'm a basic bitch white queer. If I struggled in my teen years for representation, I cannot imagine what it must have been, and still be, like for all those who didn't feel seen or represented. That's what drove me to put together *Queer Power*. I wanted to create something for the community, for the allies and for the next generation of queer youth. A book celebrating modern-day trailblazers, activists, and icons who have shaped our world and will continue to do so.

I could have gone in a number of different directions. There are a variety of amazing books out there that feature inspiring historical LGBTQ+ figures and I felt they do it so well that I didn't want to take up that space. I really could have pushed more celebrity into *Queer Power* if I wanted to, but I didn't. This book is a mix of hugely well-known public figures and some people you may not recognize. That's the charm. The people in these pages are the ones whose voices should be amplified, whose stories and journeys should be in front of you. These are people that I look up to and am inspired by. People that I have genuinely learned from.

And hope that you will, too. I couldn't fit in everyone I wanted as there are so many incredible humans out there doing the work for the LGBTQ+ community. So once you've finished the book, and reread it, and lent it to your auntie Carol, you can get out there and research other voices that need to be heard!

So, no matter where you are on your journey in life, I hope reading about these inspirational icons helps you. This book is a safe space for you, a place to lose yourself in its artwork and remind you to always live your authentically queer truth. I'm here for you.

For me, *Queer Power* isn't just a book full of idols; it's my own love letter to the LGBTQ+ community. I love you.

DOM€INK

PRONOUNS

All pronouns (she/her, he/him, they/them) in this book are the primary pronouns the icon uses.

CHAPTER ONE

OUT, PROUD,

AND VISIBLE

It's our first chapter and you're about to meet so many incredible humans. Are you ready, hun? These next few pages are looking at people who are out there and visibly representing not just the LGBTQ+ community but others, too. I don't think you can finish reading this without feeling proud of them and what they stand for!

LIL NAS X

Anyone who primarily wears cowboy hats, studded jackets, and neon boots so effortlessly, basically is ICONIC in my eyes. In August 2019, "Old Town Road," a country rap song, sat atop the Billboard 100 for nineteen weeks, the longest any single had stayed at number one since the chart began in 1958. Furthermore, Nas came out as gay while the single was dominating the charts at number one, therefore making him the only person to do so at the same time as having a number-one record. Historic.

After coming out, Nas revealed on Twitter that he thought he'd made it obvious with his rainbow-themed album cover and the lyrics on his track "C7osure." While he received a homophobic backlash from parts of the hip-hop community, Nas also had a lot of amazing support, with many fans who were Black and queer pointing out how inspiring it was to see a Black queer man succeeding in mainstream music. Then, in 2021, Lil Nas X basically did the biggest cultural reset EVER by releasing his chart smash, "MONTERO (Call Me By Your Name)," an unapologetically queer anthem with a music video featuring him pole dancing into hell and giving Satan a lap dance, all in eight-inch heels. A SERVE.

Since coming out, Nas has released more top hits, modeled for Rihanna's Fenty Beauty, won awards, and was named by *TIME* magazine as one of "the 25 most influential people on the Internet." He also still wears his signature looks, which incorporate queerness with camp humor, some futuristic aspects, and a whole lot of attitude.

ANICK SONI

The intersex community are massively underrepresented and their voices and stories need to be heard. In 2020 alone, there was a huge call to end unnecessary surgery on intersex children without their consent: The Ann & Robert H. Lurie Children's Hospital of Chicago was the first hospital to apologize for performing such surgeries in the past.

Anick Soni is at the forefront of intersex campaigning and activism. His many achievements include receiving the *GAY TIMES* Honour for British Community Trailblazer Award in 2019. Yes, Anick! Having helped to organize UK Black Pride, Pride in London, AND the first intersex march, Anick is taking huge steps in advocating for the intersex community.

His visibility and words have been huge contributors to helping representation, and he openly encourages conversations around intersex people, especially in the media. This is mirrored in Anick's FANTASTIC documentary for BBC Radio 1, "The Intersex Diaries," which charts his own journey to surgery and is powerful, beautiful, and informative. I encourage anyone who reads this to watch it straight away. Like, right now, please.

"YOU'VE HEARD THE PHRASE, 'I WEAR MY HEART ON MY SLEEVE', WELL, I KINDA WEAR MY PENIS ON MINE"

BLAIR IMANI

Blair Imani is a queer Muslim, historian, author, and activist. I think Blair plays a very important part in the queer community and the push for social justice. She came out in June 2017, while on Tucker Carlson's Fox News show talking about safe spaces for Muslims in the United States. This was a real turning point and a massive moment of visibility for the Muslim members of the LGBTQ+ community. There is a common misconception that many Muslim people are homophobic. This outdated stereotype completely erases the idea that you can be queer and Muslim, not to mention the experiences of many queer Muslim people who very much exist!

Following the program, she also wrote a blog post about her coming out and the importance of representation of queer Muslims in mainstream media. This led to an outpouring of messages of support, with many people thankful that they finally felt seen and heard. Reflecting on Instagram, she wrote: "Sure, since coming out I've been ostracized and lost opportunities but Alhamdulillah being an out and proud Muslim is a blessing that every closeted person of faith deserves to experience." Blair uses online platforms to further educate her audience on a number of issues surrounding anti-racism, LGBTQ+ people, and feminism. Her "Smarter in Seconds" video series is the highlight of my week, and I can guarantee after fifteen seconds, you will have learned not just something, but something *valuable*.

NIKKIE

With over 13.6 million followers on YouTube, *NikkieTutorials*, aka Nikkie de Jager, is one of the leading trans figures on social media and in the beauty industry. A supremely talented makeup artist, Nikkie can serve a fierce face of any kind of glam. In January 2020, she came out as trans in her video, "I'm Coming Out," which has had 35 million views and a ton of support, virtual cuddles, and love. Coming out for many trans people is a huge thing to do, and this was definitely the case for Nikkie. In her video, she revealed she had been blackmailed by someone and came out as a result of not wanting to live in fear. As she said on *The Ellen Show*, "Plot twist, that didn't happen!"

While it wasn't ideal, coming out in this way took the power away from the blackmailer. Since releasing the video, Nikkie has received unanimous support from celebrities, brands, and followers. She now openly speaks on video about her trans journey, each time constantly reminding any trans youth out there that are still afraid that "as long as I get to be myself and inspire little 'Nikkies' to be their selves, that's all I can do."

DE JAGER
"IF YOU FEEL YOU'RE TRAPPED AND THERE'S NO WAY OUT—KNOW THAT IT GETS BETTER"

ARIANA

I actually don't know how to write about my utter adoration for Ariana DeBose. I first came across her while watching the musical film *The Prom*, playing a queer character, Alyssa Greene. Then, I saw her in *West Side Story*. THEN I saw her become the first openly queer actor of color to win an Oscar for Best Supporting Actress. A historic win in so many ways! Also, she served a look that night in a Maison Valentino red trouser suit with sleeves that were giving me DRAMA and WINNER. If you haven't come across Ariana yet, I encourage you to watch her in, well, anything. In every role she plays, her versatility as an actress shines through, and she has a presence onscreen that's unparalleled.

Being an openly queer actress of color in Hollywood must not be easy. A large number of actors stay "closeted" in order to appease film studios, agents, and bosses, and to have more longevity in their career. Ariana subverts that by taking on dynamic and challenging characters. Being open about her sexuality in the press has led Ariana to inspire so many LGBQTIA+ people out there who also want to act, be open, and live freely.

As she took to the Oscars stage to accept her award, she said, "Imagine this little girl in the back seat of a white Ford Focus. Look into her eyes: You see an openly queer woman of color, an Afro-Latina, who found her strength in life through art. That's what I believe we're here to celebrate."

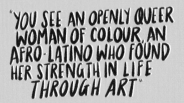

"YOU SEE AN OPENLY QUEER WOMAN OF COLOUR, AN AFRO-LATINO WHO FOUND HER STRENGTH IN LIFE THROUGH ART"

TESS HOLLIDAY

In 2013, Tess started her #effyourbeautystandards movement on Instagram, which is all about promoting body positivity, inclusivity, and, importantly, the idea that you DON'T have to be a certain size to love your body. YAS. She launched her latest fashion line based around the movement in August 2020, in collaboration with Fashion to Figure, and I am in awe of how beautifully diverse it is. She had plus-size models who were Black, trans, and disabled. Yes, inclusivity. We love to see it.

Aside from gracing the covers of magazines and being a model and an author, Tess is also very passionate about her activism. She constantly speaks up about LGBTQ+ rights, racism, ableism, and more on her social media and uses her platform to raise so much awareness for these key issues. Her raw honesty and direct approach are what make people love her (me included, times a million).

Speaking in 2019 about coming out as pansexual, she said, "I can connect with people on a more intimate level than I was before, because I don't have to pretend to be someone I'm not."

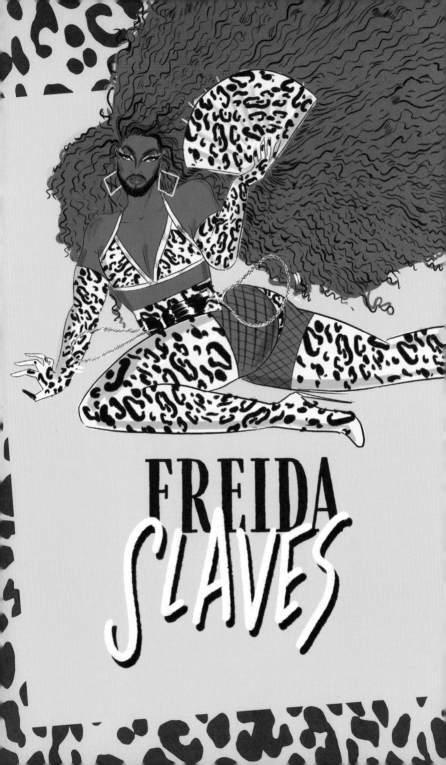

East London queen Freida Slaves is a fierce force to be reckoned with. I actually had the absolute pleasure of seeing Freida perform last year and, OH MY CHER, she was incredible. Inspired by Janet Jackson, Beyoncé, Paula Abdul, and Madonna, Freida exudes fierceness, and she KNOWS how to control a room. She was also a professional dancer, so you know that choreo is nailed tight.

Drag performers are a huge part of the LGBTQ+ community. Their performances and appearances are not always just about lip sync but also touch on raising awareness of key issues and how we as a community can unite against them. Freida is no exception. Any time she is interviewed, she always uses the opportunity to speak up about the lack of representation of Black drag queens and drag queens of color and how her visibility speaks so much to the marginalized members of our rainbow family.

Speaking to *HISKIND* magazine, she said, ". . . the more I spread the word and showcase myself, the more queens of colour will emerge." This is so important, and it's really crucial that we all continue to support and uplift these voices so they can keep creating and entertaining us with their talents.

"YOU SEE A BLACK DRAG QUEEN, JUST LIVING HER BEST LIFE"

"NORMALISE DISABLED BODIES. NORMALISE TRANS BODIES. NORMALISE PEOPLE LOOKING HOWEVER THE FHHK THEY WANT"

"People are always so hyper-focused on how a disabled person or a trans person is supposed to look or act. I'm gonna need you to throw that idea in the trash," writes Julian Gavino on a post on his Instagram, with him sat in his wheelchair, eyes closed, a soft red cardigan draped over his arms, ripped striped jeans covering his legs, as his long locks of hair sit on his shoulders. Deconstructing prejudices on how disabled and trans people are viewed and also serving a look? WERK.

Hailing from Florida, Julian Gavino is a trans-masc, disabled, awesome human who is an activist, writer, life coach, and model. He was born with Ehlers-Danlos syndrome, which affects the connective tissues in his body. While also navigating life as a trans person, Julian makes sure he uses his platform and the work he gets with brands to write and speak about the importance of trans AND disabled bodies. Through his activism, he has spoken about how important it is for queer people with overlapping identities to be recognized: "At the end of the day, it doesn't matter if there are ten million LGBTQIA+ disabled folx or five in the entire world. Those people still need representation."

ALEXANDER LEON

Alexander Leon is a writer, campaigner, and activist. His work centers on diversity, inclusion, LGBTQ+ rights, anti-racism, and mental health. He also has the most adorable Australian accent ever—warm, comforting, and like an audio hug. Alexander consistently tweets and posts about racism within the LGBTQ+ community and how we can identify it and challenge it.

His post, "Why Is Racism a Queer Issue," highlights this in the opening slide: "White LGBTQ+ people have a responsibility to understand the effect of anti-blackness and other forms of racism in our community." This is further highlighted by the small backlash Alexander has to deal with whenever he posts something like this—we have so much more work to do as a community to actively be anti-racist. I would also suggest checking out Alexander's Twitter, as his tweets are SO on point. He manages to deconstruct hypermasculinity and performative masculinity, and speaks to me on so many emotional levels in 250 characters or less in the space of three minutes. There's a power in that.

"JUST BECAUSE THE WORLD IS STILL CATCHING UP TO OUR GREATNESS, DOESN'T MEAN YOU WEREN'T ALWAYS GREAT"

MICHAELA JAÉ RODRIGUEZ

When I first started watching the tv show *Pose*, I was constantly in awe of Michaela Jaé Rodriguez's incredible acting skills. Her role as house mother, Blanca Evangelista, not only conveyed fierceness and vulnerability, but she was, for me and many other viewers, the heart of the show. Michaela Jaé's character held others together, supported them, and stood up for them. This led to Michaela Jaé becoming the first trans performer to be nominated for a lead acting Emmy, in 2021, as well as the first trans woman to WIN a Golden Globe for Best Actress in 2022! Incredible.

Michaela Jaé Rodriguez is also an iconic stage performer, having appeared in productions of *Rent*, *Runaways*, and *Street Children*. In 2019, she became the first trans woman of color to play the role of Audrey in an off-Broadway production of *Little Shop of Horrors*. When I tell you that her rendition of "Suddenly Seymour" is mind-blowingly stunnylicious, I'm not lying! I watch that performance at least once weekly. An incredible singer, Michaela Jaé has also released her first solo single, "Something to Say," which has got ALL the feel-good vibes. The video, choreo, and looks are on point, and it's a perfect slice of musical perfection for your ears.

While there wasn't a televised ceremony of the Golden Globes in 2022, Michaela Jaé took to her social media to share a message on her historic win: "They will see a young Black Latina girl from Newark, New Jersey, who had a dream to change the minds others would with love," she wrote. "Love wins."

28

"THEY WILL SEE A YOUNG BLACK LATINA GIRL FROM NEWARK, NEW JERSEY, WHO HAD A DREAM, TO CHANGE THE MINDS OTHERS WOULD WITH *LOVE*"

"I WILL ALWAYS WANT TO BE HONEST ABOUT MY OWN EXPERIENCES"

RINA SAWAYAMA

A Japanese-British singer-songwriter, Rina Sawayama is the pansexual queer pop icon the world needs right now. Her debut album, *Sawayama*, is packed full of songs about self-expression and sexuality, and is a full-on queertastic experience in every way. Previously identifying as bisexual, Rina came out as pansexual in 2018 in *Vice* magazine: "For me there's still a lack of representation. I just think the reason I wasn't so comfortable with my sexuality was because there was no one on TV or anywhere that I could point to and go, 'Look, Mom! This person is what I was talking about!'"

Rina used this moment to discuss the deeper themes of her lyrics, past experiences, and her identity. She was also fully aware of how people would view her, as she was in a heterosexual relationship at the time. Her song "Cherry" touches on this viewpoint, that bi and pan people "don't feel authentically queer when they're in heterosexual relationships." I think it's really important to say here that no matter where you are on your queer journey, or who you're with, *every* part of you deserves and should be accepted by a queer safe space. Always. On that note, go stream "Cherry" now.

ARUN BLAIR-MANGAT

Arun Blair-Mangat, or A.B.M., as I like to call him, is an incredible genderqueer actor, composer, and talented singer of notes no-human-can-ever-reach, especially me (I have tried numerous times).

In 2019, he starred in *& Juliet*, a revisionist musical based on the story of Shakespeare's *Romeo and Juliet*. His character is the nonbinary character, May, one of the many large supporting characters in the ensemble piece. May's journey is central to the story of *& Juliet*. What I love about A.B.M. is how he has worked so hard to make sure he represents the nonbinary community correctly and sensitively. When I went to see the show, it was the first time I'd seen a gender nonconforming main character in a musical in London's West End. A.B.M. has a talent for holding the audience captive while educating them at the same time.

As he said to *Attitude* magazine in February 2020, "This is the most that I've loved myself in a long time because I'm so satiated by this show."

"IT ALLOWS ME TO EMBRACE MY OTHERNESS; IT CELEBRATES THAT"

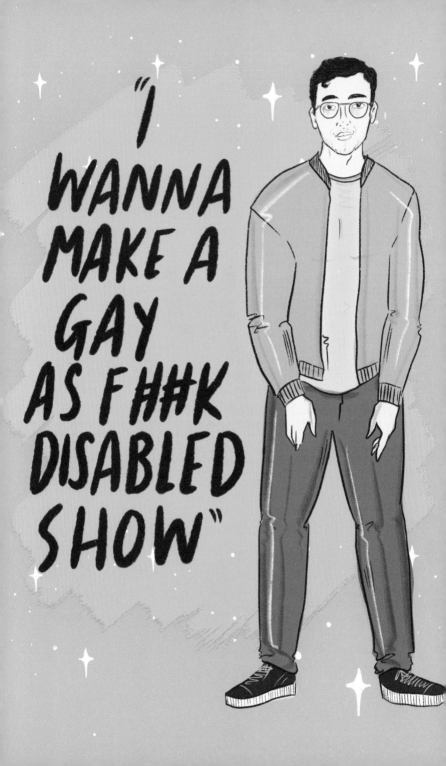

RYAN O'CONNELL

I remember sitting down to watch *Special* on Netflix and then spending the following three hours feeling a multitude of emotions. It's funny, it's sad, it's progressive AF. It's just amazing. So, if you haven't watched it yet, I advise you do. The show relates to viewers on multiple levels, while also incorporating themes of body positivity, mental health, queer rights, and ableism, too.

The lead character is played by Ryan O'Connell, the writer and creator of the series. It's a semi-autobiographical take on O'Connell's own life story—navigating being queer and having cerebral palsy while living in LA. Originally, O'Connell didn't think *Special* would happen. Speaking to *Deadline* he said, "It was really, really hard to sell a show with a gay, disabled lead, quite frankly, so we had to take a lot of different pathways to getting it made." *Special* is now an Emmy-nominated show, which is a massive achievement, especially in the movement for representation of the disabled community in the media. The LGBTQ+ community is so vast and varied, and shows like *Special* are so important in order that every part of the rainbow feels valid and visible.

THINGS TO CONSIDER WHEN COMING OUT:

Firstly, only come out when YOU are ready. No one should ever tell you how or when to come out; that's something that only you will know. If you don't feel the timing is right, then don't do it—that's okay! When you do decide that the time is right, here are some tips to help you slam those closet doors wide open. If you've done this already or you're not queer, share these tips with people in your life who might need them.

1. YOU DON'T NEED TO LABEL YOURSELF

Whatever stage you're at in your journey, you really don't need to label yourself. Some people come out as gay, then through experiences and life, realize they're bisexual or pan, or whatever they want to identify as sexually. "Queer" is an inclusive term that can be used for a number of sexualities. Don't feel pressured to label yourself; there's only one YOU and that's what makes you so unique.

2. GENDER ROLES

So—and this could do with a whole book in itself—please leave those preconceived ideas of gender tucked away somewhere. You just need to forget the ideas that the woman in the relationship does this and the man does that. The beauty of the queer community is that there are so many different variations of relationships, and what you want for yours doesn't need to be set around very old views of gender. Keep an open mind and embrace anything.

3. LEARN SOME SHIT

The LGBTQ+ community has a history of queer rights, fights for equality, and important figures. Read up on some icons who paved the way. Learning LGBTQ+ history is a privilege. It will remind you how far we have come and the struggles we've faced. LGBTQ+ rights are not equal everywhere, so consider this when thinking about how you can support others.

4. CONFIDE IN SOMEONE

Telling a friend first and actually vocalizing how you feel is a great step forward in coming out to others. I remember telling a friend and the burden immediately felt a little less heavy. Make sure it's someone who knows you and that you can trust them with your little queer heart. If you're really nervous about telling a friend, I'd suggest talking to someone on a queer helpline first. Take your time and take it steady. Don't rush yourself.

5. WERK THAT CLUB

If you're coming out and this affects your life at school, I'd suggest enquiring about whether there is an LGBTQ+ Alliance Club. Most schools should have something like this, so maybe reach out to them and ask about their experiences being queer at school. Also, new queer friends. YAY.

6. BE SOCIAL AND SAFE

On your social media, follow, share, and repost queer creators. You don't have to make your whole feed rainbowlicious, but following a few LGBTQ+ accounts you can personally relate to or feel seen by is a great reminder that you are valid, loved, and there are people out there doing their thing, and you can, TOO. Curate your social media to be an online safe space. If you don't follow me, I won't be offended . . . *goes and cries in gay listening to Sinead O' Connor*.

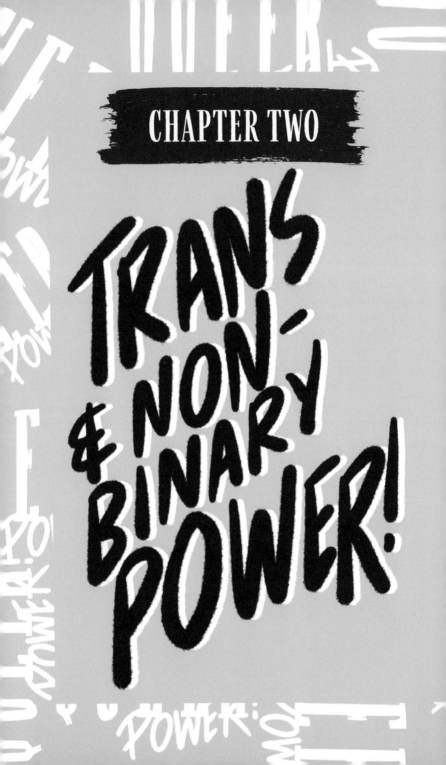

CHAPTER TWO

TRANS NON-BINARY & POWER!

The trans and nonbinary community make up a hugely important part of the LGBTQ+ family. Unfortunately, not everywhere in the world sees it that way and the "T" of the LGBTQ+ needs more support and love than ever. Gender is a spectrum, and while the word "trans" is an adjective that is often used as an umbrella term, "nonbinary" describes people who do not identify within the margins of the gender binary (man and woman). The following are icons who are out there, actively pushing for more trans representation and fighting for their rights and for justice at the same time.

DOMINIQUE JACKSON

Tobagonian American actress, model, and real-life ballroom queen, Dominique Jackson is known to most for her role of Elektra on television's *Pose*. If you haven't seen it yet, where have you been, hun? An original ballroom legend herself, Dominique cemented her status in the House of Sinclair in NYC. She pursued different modeling gigs and acting opportunities and eventually landed a role in *Pose*, a show set in the late 1980s that focuses on the ballroom scene. The show made history for having the largest cast of transgender actors playing transgender characters.

Having since become a pop culture and queer icon, Dominique has also used her voice for the trans community, openly talking about her experiences growing up and working with many different LGBTQ+ charities and organizations. Her passionate speech at the Human Rights Campaign's National Dinner in 2019 is really powerful and a must-watch.

CHELLA MAN

Having documented his transition on YouTube to more than four million viewers, Chella Man is the deaf, Chinese and Jewish activist the world needs right now. Chella uses his continually growing space on YouTube for open conversation around his relationships, art, activism, and more. At just twenty-one years old, he has been a TEDx speaker, modeled for Calvin Klein, and starred as a DC superhero in *Titans*. He uses his YouTube videos and Instagram posts to speak up for the LGBTQ+ disabled community and advocate for their need to have their voices heard and seen. This is also documented in Chella's book, *Continuum*.

Chella Man is also the FIRST trans-masculine and deaf person to sign with IMG Models. Working as a model and actor, he also pushes for better visibility for disabled queer performers. Speaking to *Vogue*, he quite rightly said, "Overall, until disabled, queer BIPoC representation mirrors how the world is as it is, true inclusivity is yet to be reached." Chella also documents and shares his relationship with his partner, MaryV Benoit. It's beautiful and adorable and so needed. We need to see more queer love!

KENNY ETHAN JONES

Kenny Ethan Jones is a transgender model and activist and all-round awesome human. What I think makes Kenny really important is that he openly speaks up and talks about trans and gender nonconforming people who menstruate.

I hadn't really seen this topic covered outside cis bodies much (well, ever) until I FOUND Kenny. He gained attention in 2018 as the first transgender man to front a UK period campaign from Pink Parcel. This was a huge turning point and made history. The fact that Kenny was even in that campaign will have helped, and will continue to help, so that many trans and gender nonconforming people have someone to relate to and represent them. Since then, Kenny has been on the cover of magazines, and he talks frequently about body politics, mental health, and intimacy. One of my favorite quotes of his is this: "You don't have to be the toxic masculinity of manhood to be valid as a man."

JUNO DAWSON

Juno Dawson is a trans author and actress from Yorkshire, England. To date, she has written around twenty books and is basically a book machine (I'm not complaining—every book she has authored is fantastic and carries an important message for the reader!). She is also often found taking part in different trans rights marches—she puts it best herself on her Instagram: "So once again, I am spending a Saturday screaming at Parliament because it feels like the right thing to do."

We're living in a time where trans rights are frequently under attack and it's crucial we have figures like Juno taking up space and talking about their experiences. It's also imperative that we keep supporting trans writers and their books. Juno's work, and Juno herself, speaks to and relates to so many trans and queer people out there. And she does it all so well in a sequin blazer, too. Her latest young adult book, *Wonderland*, features a trans lead character, which proves you can have a best-selling book for teens without needing a boy wizard. So far, the book has been a best seller, had numerous rave reviews, and been featured as part of the Zoella Book Club. All while during a pandemic. I bow to you, Queen Juno!

"I AM A WOMAN BECAUSE I AM A WOMAN AND I'VE KNOWN THAT SINCE I WAS OLD ENOUGH TO KNOW"

ALOK VAID-MENON

Alok is an Indian American, trans feminine writer and activist. Texas-born and based in New York, they have become a staple in the online LGBTQ+ community for their extensive work around equality for gender nonconforming people. All of Alok's captions carry a resonance and weight. They were vocal about the Black Lives Matter movement in 2020, speaking on Black Trans Lives and all the work we still have to do to challenge racism and transphobia.

Alok also consistently keeps the conversation going around gender, through their public appearances, social media, and their books, *Beyond the Gender Binary* (2020) and *Your Wound/My Garden* (2021). In a world where more and more people identify as nonbinary, Alok continues to use their platform to give this community a voice. They encourage their audience to embrace all ideas of gender and what gender is. "One gender, one aesthetic, one medium, one field . . . Things are so much more fluid than that. I fundamentally believe in cross-pollination," they told *GQ*.

"I HAVE FOUND BEAUTY IN SO MANY PLACES WHERE I WAS TAUGHT SHAME, MY FRIENDSHIPS ARE DEEP & VULNERABLE, I KNOW FIRMLY & IRREVOCABLY WHO I AM"

RADAM RIDWAN

Lots of people created social media side-hustles during the 2020 lockdown. Radam Ridwan was no exception. Radam created the online #lockdownlookbook where they posted a full fashion look to their Instagram grid every single day, for the whole of lockdown. I'm talking platform boots, tassels, sequins, bits of nudity. EVERYTHING. They also have an amazing collection of hats. Looks like these made my day—and a whole lot of other people's—a lot more glamorous. Radam interspersed these posts with thoughtfully written words on fighting transphobia, ultimately creating different calls to action on how to support the gender nonconforming and trans community.

While Radam knows how to serve a look, their words on their experiences of how they are treated day-to-day are a somber reminder that we need to keep supporting and protecting our nonbinary folk against threats. We have to keep on raising their voices online and offline so that they can be heard.

"THE BIG PROBLEM FOR NON-BINARY PEOPLE LIKE ME ISN'T JUST BEING SEEN—IT'S BEING SEEN AS HUMAN"

"I DON'T KNOW WHO I AM
OUTSIDE OF SOMEONE
WHO'S JUST TRYING TO BE
FREE AND FIND SAFETY FOR
MYSELF AND OTHERS"

INDYA MOORE

Named one of *TIME* magazine's 100 Most Influential People in 2019, Indya Moore is a transgender nonbinary force of awesomeness. Indya left home at fourteen and grew up in foster care. They worked as a sex worker and went through drug addiction, homelessness, and hormone treatment. They managed to overcome these experiences and channel them into their role as Angel on *Pose*. The show became a huge success and Indya became an overnight name, one of the most prominent faces for a transgender nonbinary person of color on television and in the public eye.

Since then, Indya has modeled for Calvin Klein and Louis Vuitton, and made their runway debut at New York Fashion Week 2020 for Jason Wu. In June 2020, in honor of the fiftieth anniversary of the first LGBTQ Pride march, *Queerty* named them among the fifty queer heroes "leading the nation toward equality, acceptance, and dignity for all people." Indya always takes the opportunity to speak about their activism work around trans rights. Speaking to the E! channel on the red carpet at the 2019 Emmys, Indya was vocal about the importance of trans people in fashion spaces, such as their own work as an ambassador for Louis Vuitton. They said, "It's more tricky to exist than to walk in this dress."

DANIELA VEGA

Daniela Vega is a Chilean actress mostly known for her career-defining, award-winning role in *A Fantastic Woman*. She was the FIRST transgender person in history to present an award at the Academy Awards ceremony, in 2018. Taking to the stage, ruffles galore and elegance personified in a pink fuchsia gown by Maria Lucia Hohan, she addressed the crowd, asking them to "open their hearts." *TIME* magazine coined the moment by naming Daniela the "Breakout Oscars Star" of that year.

A Fantastic Woman won the Oscar for Best Foreign Language Film and drew international attention to Daniela. This was a turning point for transgender rights in Chile and helped push forward a bill (from 2013) for trans people to legally change their names and gender on official documents. This bill eventually took effect in 2019 with Daniela reflecting on her Instagram and sharing a message of support: "I dedicate this day to the beautiful conquest of ruling the name."

"I WANT TO INVITE YOU TO OPEN YOUR HEARTS AND YOUR FEELINGS TO FEEL THE REALITY, TO FEEL LOVE. CAN YOU FEEL IT?"

CHARLIE CRAGGS

Founder of Nail Transphobia, author and self-proclaimed "bad bitch," Charlie Craggs runs pop-up nail salons across the UK, where she and her team of trans and nonbinary nail technicians are there to buff, polish, and educate you on trans rights and activism, while also serving you some nailtastic art to serve and slay with.

In 2017, she released her book *To My Trans Sisters*—an anthology of one hundred letters by trans women, about and FOR trans women. The book was nominated for a number of awards and was also a finalist in the thirtieth Lambda Literary Awards.

Described as the "Voice of a community" by *Vogue* (OMG! right?), Charlie Craggs is never afraid to speak her mind and call out brands, public figures, and others on transphobia. What I love about Charlie is that she is always authentically herself and does not and will not change for anyone. She openly talks about her surgeries, dating, sex, and more on social media, and I myself have learned SO much from her.

In 2018, Charlie was part of a campaign for inclusion of a transgender rainbow flag in Unicode, which was added to the standard emoji listing in 2020. YES, CHARLIE. TRANS RIGHTS!

JANET MOCK

I absolutely live for Janet Mock. She's an award-winning writer, producer, director, queen of EVERYTHING. Aside from that, she's also a *New York Times* best-selling author for her books, *Redefining Realness* and *Surpassing Certainty*.

With a career in journalism, working as a staff editor for *People* magazine's website, Janet came out publicly as trans in a *Marie Claire* article. While she didn't write the article, she didn't like how the magazine represented her and how her story was told with the magazine stating she was born and raised as a boy, even though Janet has always been a girl. Eventually, after releasing her best seller, *Redefining Realness*, she became a contributing editor at *Marie Claire*. Werk!

In 2018, Mock made history as the first trans woman of color hired as a writer and director for a TV series, *Pose*! Speaking about her experience in the early days of production of the show, she said, "I watch the monitors sometimes . . . with tears in my eyes, realizing that these were the sort of stories that I was craving as a young person."

THEN, in 2019, Mock made even more history when she signed her deal with Netflix, making her the first trans person to "sign a production pact with a major studio." This means Janet can write, direct, and create her own projects on a major streaming site.

Aside from bringing much-needed trans representation in front of and behind the camera to the television and film industry, Janet has also adorned the cover of *Harpers Bazaar*, *Marie Claire*, *VOGUE*, and *Entertainment Weekly*. She regularly works with fashion house Maison Valentino, and continually serves chic and luxuriously gorgeous high-end looks on the red carpet.

CRYSTAL
RASMUSSEN

Crystal Rasmussen is a nonbinary drag performer, author, writer, and an absolute ICON in London. They combine a sharp wit, the vocal range of Mariah Carey, and the thigh-high snakeskin boots of my dreams. A multitalented performer, Crystal took their one-queen show, *The Bible 2*, to the world's largest arts festival, Edinburgh Fringe, and London and received rave reviews. They also host *Dragony Aunts* for Comedy Central. On top of that, Crystal also wrote the brilliantly funny *Diary of a Drag Queen*, their semi-autobiographical book on their own queer experiences that take place over a year. Basically, Crystal can do anything and everything.

When I first met Crystal, I was taken in by how glamorous they were, how funny they were, but also how kind they were. There's something in Crystal's big blue eyes that just makes you feel at home and loved. Magical humans like Crystal are very hard to come by in this world, and they always promote a message of inclusivity and self-love.

"UR POWER RADIATES AND UR FLUIDITY IN WHATEVER FORM IS NOT ONLY VALID, IT'S BEAUTIFUL"

HOW TO BE AN ALLY TO THE TRANS & NONBINARY COMMUNITY:

As a white queer, I have no space to talk about what it's like to transition or come out as trans or gender nonconforming. However, I can help you become an ally to the trans community, which is especially vulnerable right now. If you're reading this and aren't cis, and you think it would help, please show these pages to loved ones. Maybe take a pic or lend the book, share with friends, and spread the word of trans allyship! Yes!

1. DONATE

There are trans funds/mutual aids and charities you can support with as little as a fiver. That money goes a long way. You could do a one-off payment or even set up a standing order. If that's not financially viable, perhaps share the link on your socials so other people who can afford to can help out. Better yet, organize a fundraiser! There are people transitioning, needing surgeries, or therapy across the world 24/7, so anything you can do to help them get closer to what they need is amazing.

2. SIGN AND SHARE

There are petitions all over social media relating to government bills, fighting for equality for trans people, and justice for the families of trans people who have been killed. These are important to show those in power the outrage at what is going on. With enough signatures, we can get justice! Stick a link in your bio, start a WhatsApp chain—keep sharing.

3. SUPPORT TRANS AND NONBINARY CREATORS

Social media is FULL of trans and nonbinary creators, authors, actors, singers, and more. However, not all big brands will approach them and involve them with work outside of Pride season. Follow them, like them, share their work with your followers. These people need to be seen and their stories need to be heard. Go watch their YouTube videos, buy their T-shirts, and read their books. Whatever you do will go directly toward helping them and letting them know they have support out there.

4. TALK IT OUT

There may be situations where a friend, a family member, or in my case once, a date, is being "problematic" in their views on trans people. These are moments for this person to learn and grow, so have a conversation with them about what they've said and how that affects the larger community. I've had awkward conversations with people where I've pulled them up on something and a year later, I've seen them pull someone else up on their words around trans and nonbinary people. More of this, please.

5. SUPPORT TRANS AUTHORS

Read trans authors! Read books with trans characters! The publishing industry needs more representation in terms of trans writing and the best way to let them know is by buying their books, tweeting how much you love them, and supporting the authors.

6. START LEARNING

There are numerous lists on the Internet for learning more about the history of trans and nonbinary people. There are books, films, documentaries, podcasts, songs, and more! Shows like *Pose* are gateways for cis people to learn and see what has to be done going forward. Don't stop at one show; consume as much information as you can.

CHAPTER THREE

PROUD FAMILIES

These are icons that come from a wide range of different families—a family doesn't always need to be blood related. As queer people, we have a lot to navigate with our family; sometimes it's good, sometimes not so good. With that, there is a special power in discovering your "chosen" family! This chapter also touches on allies for the queer community and what they've done to help fight for LGBTQ+ rights.

CHASE STRANGIO

Working as the Deputy Director for Transgender Justice for the American Civil Liberties Union's LGBT & HIV Project, Chase Strangio is a lawyer and trans-rights activist! Yes! Come through, trans lawyer representation!

While working for the ACLU, Chase has been part of the legal team that has helped the LGBTQ+ community receive justice after facing ignorance and prejudice, including *Bostock v. Clayton County*, a 2020 landmark case where the US Supreme Court ruled that it is illegal to discriminate against transgender identity and sexual orientation at work.

Chase is continually vocal about issues and legislation queer and trans people face in the United States. With Florida's "Don't Say Gay" bill and other bills in Idaho and Texas that are directly affecting trans youth, Chase utilizes his platform on social media and in the press to bring awareness to these issues. He also provides information and educates people on how they can help by launching their own campaigns to "build power and support for trans young people and the organizers and communities fighting alongside them."

Alongside activist and writer Raquel Willis, Chase launched Trans Week of Visibility and Action (TWOVA) in 2021. With campaigns focused on Transgender Day of Visibility (March 31), Trans Week also provides resources for trans people to use over the year to combat trans hate and anti-trans legislation.

CHOUDREY

In Sabah Choudrey's own words, they're a "reluctant activist on most things trans, brown and hairy." Speaker, writer, and performer, Sabah is also the Head of Youth Services at Gendered Intelligence and cofounder of Colours Youth UK, an organisation that helps Black and PoC queer youth navigate their experiences through workshops, mentoring schemes, and more. Safe spaces like these are essential for those who are marginalized within the LGBTQ+ community, to remind them they have a chosen family and also to celebrate who they are and how far they have come.

As a trans youth worker for Gendered Intelligence, Sabah has been vocal about trans rights and how important it is we keep fighting for the trans youth of tomorrow. They provide downloadable resources and content on their website so anyone can educate themselves on how to support and be an ally. Furthermore, they put all of this information together in their first book, *Supporting Trans People of Colour: How to Make Your Practice Inclusive*. What a legend.

"THE WORK WE DO ON OURSELVES IS AS IMPORTANT AS THE WORK WE DO FOR OUR YOUNG PEOPLE"

THE UNION/ WADE FAMILY

Daughter of actress Gabrielle Union and retired NBA star Dwyane Wade, thirteen-year-old Zaya Wade, came out as trans in early 2020. Both parents publicly spoke out so well about their daughter's experience, they are a shining example of how to act when someone you love comes out as trans. Dwyane even went as far as designing some custom Pride trainers for his daughter.

"We're just trying to figure out as much information as we can to make sure that we give our child the best opportunity to be, you know, her best self," Dwyane said on *The Ellen Show*. Since then, Zaya has become an emerging figure of trans youth and had her red-carpet debut at The Truth Awards with her parents, the trio wearing a full coordinated matching ensemble. Now *that* is how you do trans allyship as parents.

"YOU ARE A LEADER. IT'S OUR OPPORTUNITY TO ALLOW YOU TO BE A VOICE" DWYANE WADE

"I'M JUST CONSTANTLY TRYING TO LEARN AND NOT SPEAK FOR OTHER PEOPLE, BUT SPEAK WITH THEM. THAT'S A BIG PART OF MY ALLY JOURNEY"

JADE THIRLWALL

ALLY Alert

Jade Thirlwall is a member of internationally acclaimed girl group Little Mix. Not only is she a total queen, she is also a fantastic ally to the LGBTQ+ community. Using her platform and through her role as a Stonewall UK ambassador, she consistently speaks up for queer rights and trans rights, taking part in marches, protests, and sharing valuable information with her followers. With such an engaged following, Jade is showing her audience HOW to be an ally and help raise LGBTQ+ voices up and support these movements in an authentic way.

In an interview with *Attitude*, she said, "I've really tried to find ways of, like I've said before, walking the walk instead of just talking the talk, and really trying to show them that I'm doing all that I can to help." I, for one, truly value the honest and passionate work Jade does for the community by speaking up for us *and* showing up. She also serves a fierce leotard and fan combo lewk, am I right? Now, go stream some Little Mix in your kitchen, please.

TETE BANG

TeTe Bang is a DJ and female drag performer and the star of drag makeover show *Drag SOS*. As a female drag queen, TeTe has her existence and drag artistry questioned just because of her gender. This really shouldn't be happening these days, but some people need a reminder—so, in case you're reading this and thinking that, just check yourself, hun, because drag is art and drag is for EVERYONE, not just cis men.

Every look TeTe creates is a playful eleganza of color, camp, and pink, and she designs and makes a lot of them herself. During lockdown, she even created "TeTe's Tutorials," short draggy D.I.Y. videos on how to add volume to wigs, create headdresses, sew dresses, and more! Excuse me while I go and attempt to make a custom gogo dress with matching headdress . . .

"I WAS FORTUNATE ENOUGH TO BE BROUGHT UP AROUND STRONG WOMEN WHO TAUGHT ME TO BE BOLD AND EXPRESS HOW I FEEL"

LADY GAGA

She's Mother Monster. She's Queen of Chromatica. She's a total queer symbol of joy and hope and is solely responsible for shoulder pads and peplums making a comeback in 2008. She's Lady Gaga! Musician, writer, actress, and many other things, Gaga has been a solid supporter of the LGBTQ+ community throughout her many years of stardom.

Here's a brief overview—she organized her fans to help volunteer in supporting queer homeless youth at shelters across the United States, she continually fights for her LGBTQ+ fans in countries where they have no rights, such as Russia, she's spoken up about homophobia in the music industry, spoken at Stonewall rallies, and delivered us the queertastically empowering anthem, "Born This Way." For me, the most important moment was in 2011 when asked in an interview, "if she had a penis," instead of denying it, she said, "Maybe I do. Would it be so terrible?"

TANYA COMPAS

Tanya Compas is a freelance youth worker and engagement specialist. During the pandemic and at the height of the Black Lives Matter movement, Tanya founded the brilliant Exist Loudly Fund. In setting up a GoFundMe page, Tanya wanted to create a way to raise money for her workshops for Black queer youth to help them find that safe space in their lives. She also wanted to create a space where they could meet others they can relate to and form relationships with.

The GoFundMe page went viral and Tanya was featured in *Vogue* and *GAY TIMES*. Through Tanya's constant hard work and passion, she managed to raise over $100,000! Yes! Tanya shared the extra finances among other queer funds and organizations. She is a truly inspirational person for so many, especially for all the work she does with the Black and PoC queer community. These spaces are so needed right now. As she wrote on Instagram when she shared the news: "I am so happy to be able to use my social media platform to create tangible change in our communities to help queer & trans Black and PoC youth."

PABLLO VITTAR

In Brazil, LGBTQ+ rights are still under attack and homophobia even now isn't considered a crime. The country has three hundred active organizations working toward equal rights, and figures like drag queen and pop star Pabllo Vittar are so important to the movement. In 2014, after going viral singing on local TV in Brazil, Pabllo's career began to take off. Fast forward to 2020 and she has over ten million followers on Instagram, has graced the cover of many magazines, and performed at the MTV European Music Awards.

Pabllo's visibility and her message of equality have been an integral part of many interviews. She refuses to hide who she is and wants to be seen so that the queer youth in Brazil growing up have someone to look up to and aspire to. Her existence in itself is a rebellion against the Brazilian government's views toward the LGBTQ+ community. She herself said in an interview with *Vogue*, "This is what makes my job worth it, to change other people's lives, or it wouldn't be worth it."

"I'VE BEEN ENDLESSLY INSPIRED BY SO MANY IN THE TRANS COMMUNITY"

On the first of December 2020, after months of the COVID-19 pandemic and numerous attacks on the trans community, Elliot Page took to his Instagram to share something important with the world. Something that would change everything: "Hi friends," he wrote. "I want to share with you that I am trans, my pronouns are he/they and my name is Elliot."

In his message, Elliot opened up about his gender and sexuality, and his words reached millions. "I can't begin to express how remarkable it feels to finally love who I am enough to pursue my authentic self," he said. "I've been endlessly inspired by so many in the trans community. Thank you for your courage, your generosity and ceaselessly working to make this world a more inclusive and compassionate place." The whole letter itself is raw and powerful and an important take on a trans person's view on being openly trans in the current political climate.

Being an Oscar-, BAFTA-, and EMMY-nominated actor, he received unanimous support from fellow trans actors and peers in the film industry. This also led him to become the first openly trans man to appear on the cover of *Time* magazine. Furthermore, he insisted that trans photographer Wynne Neilly shoot the cover, too. What. An. ICON!

Elliot also regularly uses his platform to raise awareness, speaking with Raquel Willis and Chase Strangio for Trans Week of Visibility about trans joy, and challenging misinformation around the trans community in the media. Yes, Elliot!

DRAG
Syndrome

Gaia Callas, Lady Francesca, Horrora Shebang, and Justin Bond make up Drag Syndrome, the world's first collective of drag performers with Down syndrome, who are out there to challenge stereotypes and create a stage for people with learning disabilities. Founder and artistic director Daniel Vais runs a dance company called Culture Device that works with dancers with Down syndrome. Eventually, some of his performers expressed an interest in wanting to perform in drag. Daniel booked their first gig, something he intended to be a one-off. The gig sold out and the rest is history.

As their popularity grew, Drag Syndrome have been featured in British *Vogue* and performed at DragCon UK. Queer spaces aren't always the most accessible for disabled members of the community, so a group like Drag Syndrome are a welcome step forward in progress for representation and more inclusivity for the queer disabled community.

"ART IS VERY POWERFUL, AND ART AND CULTURE IS VERY IMPORTANT. PEOPLE WITH DOWN'S SYNDROME BRING THE HEART TO THE ART"
FOUNDER, DANIEL VAIS

It's not every day you come across a drag unicorn, but then that's what makes Cheddar Gorgeous so great. Cheddar is also a star on drag makeover show *Drag SOS* (highly recommended viewing, huns) and—plot twist ahoy—an academic who knows a whole lot of stuff about anthropology. Cheddar is at the beating heart of the Manchester LGBTQ+ community AND with their drag family, the Family Gorgeous.

With brains, sequins, and a unicorn horn, Cheddar also frequently speaks up about current issues and how we as a community can face them. At their TEDx talk (yup, Cheddar is a TEDx speaker, TOO), "The Power of Drag," they said something about drag and identity that really stuck with me: "I believe that drag is one of the most powerful forms of self-exploration, expression, and political action."

"WHETHER YOU'RE MALE, FEMALE, STRAIGHT OR GAY, OLD OR YOUNG, DRAG IS ALL ABOUT FINDING YOUR INNER MOST GLAMOROUS ROUTE TO SELF-CONFIDENCE"

JESSIE WARE

It's not every day you get an ally pop-star queen who dedicates an album as a "thank you" to the LGBTQ+ community. However, Jessie Ware did just that. In 2020, during Pride month and with the Black Lives Matter movement on the rise, Jessie released *What's Your Pleasure*, an incredible disco-infused album of power, sensuality, and tunes that make your hips wiggle. Speaking with *GAY TIMES*, she mentioned how her queer fans had embraced her music over the years and how her latest offering is a "safe space where we can dance, feel free and express yourself." She uses her huge platform to speak out about LGBTQ+ rights and remind her fans that along with her music, she is also a safe space for the community, and will continually support and be an ally to them.

Jessie released two videos for the single, also entitled "What's Your Pleasure," one a dance video featuring the incredible Black queer dancer Nicolas Huchard in a variety of wigs, heels, and outfits (honestly, you have to watch it). The second featured Jessie serving a ton of looks herself, including this uber-camp leather dress with the most over-the-top hair I have ever seen (styled by hair king Patrick Wilson). As Dolly Parton once said, "The higher the hair, the closer to God"—I truly believe this hair reached past God, past the universe, and now lives in its own queertastic dimension of awesomeness surrounded by rainbows and looks down on us with love and pride.

ALLY Alert

HOW TO BE A SUPPORT TO A QUEER PERSON:

You may not feel like this title applies to you but it does. Queer people have varying experiences of trauma, pain, and rejection, and they carry those feelings with them as they navigate life. Sure, this page is for your cis straight friends, but maybe this page is also a reminder for you on how to check in with your queer chosen family, or even yourself?

1. LISTEN

Listening is a powerful way to get to know someone. *Offering* to listen is even more powerful, as you're literally saying to someone, "You can be vulnerable with me and I'm a safe space." Sometimes a person just needs to RANT—I get that—and for you, it may feel like a lot to listen, but to the person offloading their pain, anxieties, and whatever else, that will really mean so much to them.

2. CHECK IN ON THEM

Whether someone is going through something in your group or not, I always think it's good to check in on them. If I haven't heard from someone in a few days, I'll even message them sometimes saying, "Just checking in, how you doing?" (Normally followed by a dinosaur emoji.) In some instances I'll get a reply that they're "fine," just "super busy," and in other instances they'll start to open up. The feeling that someone is thinking of you and wants to know you're okay is really quite something, so let your friends know.

3. GO TO QUEER SPACES

The amount of times growing up I had people tell me they wouldn't go to a bar because it was "gay" is off the charts. A great way to support a queer person is by going to a queer pub or show or drag night with them; it shows you want to support them and be part of their world. Also, it's guaranteed to be the BEST TIME. If you're not LGBTQ+, be aware you're taking up room in a queer space and respect that. You're always welcome in those spaces, just be aware that they exist to help queer people feel safe and are somewhere they can fully be every color of the rainbow they want to be.

4. AVOID SAYING MICROAGGRESSIONS

Have a read about things to say and not say to a queer person. People sometimes say shit that really isn't cool. When I worked in retail (for a long time), I had a lot thrown at me. Microaggressions like "You don't look gay" or "Who's the man and who's the woman" just aren't fun, and not all queer people feel comfortable answering them, so if you do say one, be sure to call yourself out, and if someone else says something, call them out, hun!

5. LET THEM KNOW YOU'RE A SAFE SPACE

It's always good in the home, workplace, or wherever, to let a queer person know YOU are a safe space for them. A place they can freely express who they are and be authentically themselves. Sometimes just literally saying, "I'm a safe space for you" is all the reassurance someone needs!

6. SHOW UP FOR THEM

This could be showing up for a queer friend's event to support or even going with them to Pride. These are moments in which your support as an ally is invaluable and won't be forgotten. Furthermore, if you can't physically get somewhere, share their posts, pictures, and work on your social channels. Raise and amplify their voices!

Queer mental health is uniquely different. We have to regularly deal with so many different emotions and feelings. Existing in the world can be quite overwhelming sometimes, but queer icons are here to remind you that you have got this, you can face it, and you can overcome it. Be kind to yourself.

QUEER SELF!

JVN

Jonathan Van Ness aka JVN is a hairdresser, author, and star of Netflix's critically acclaimed and gayalicious show *Queer Eye*. JVN identifies as nonbinary and was the first non-female to be on the cover of *Cosmopolitan* magazine in thirty-five years, come through progressivity! Appearing on *Queer Eye* as the hair and beauty expert, JVN shot to fame thanks to their totally adorable personality, sharp wit, and words of wisdom for the heroes they make over on the show. *Queer Eye* is known for its emotional moments and Jonathan does not shy away from speaking openly about their own personal journey with their mental health. Completely meme-worthy and viral AF, JVN has cemented themself as a true queer icon in pop culture.

JVN uses their podcast, *Getting Curious With Jonathan Van Ness* (now also a TV show, yay!), to promote their activism and to speak on current political and social issues in the United States. I love how knowledgeable they are about so many things. They can give you a homemade solution for dry scalp (apple cider vinegar) but also school you on every presidential candidate in American politics right now (sometimes in the same sentence!).

In November of 2019, they came out as HIV positive, with unanimous support from everyone. Having a figure like Jonathan share their status lets others in the HIV community know they are not alone.

CHAR ELLESSE

Back in 2017, Char Ellesse set up Girls Will Be Boys, a platform with a mission to challenge gender roles and deconstruct the idea of the gender binary. With this movement, Char shares experiences from women who want to tell their stories about gender identity and self-acceptance alongside the tagline: "Is it always binary?" Sitting alongside GWBB, is #omgshesbald, a short film and project she created to explore "modern ideas of femininity through women who have shaved their heads." It also highlights that women should be able to shave their heads, feel empowered, and not have their gender, sexuality, or how feminine they are questioned by others.

With a highly engaged following on social media, she uses her captions as a way to engage with her audience and start conversations around racism, queer rights, body positivity, and mental health. Talking about how she felt on World Suicide Prevention Day, Char wrote: "Whether times have been hard or still are, you deserve the help you need to keep on keeping on."

"LET YOURSELF FEEL AND YOU'LL KNOW WHAT TO DO"

LOTTIE
L'AMOUR

Lottie L'Amour is a body positive, plus-size activist and founder of Love My Chub Club, a platform that "celebrates diverse fat bodies." She's also open about her journey with her mental health and actively speaks about times when she is struggling to her audience. It's quite rare for creators on social media to be as transparent as Lottie, but by being so vulnerable to so many, she is actively helping so many other queer people (including me). In one post she wrote: "Mental health recovery is not linear. There's no magic potion to make you feel better."

Lottie has won numerous awards for work she has done online and offline around mental health and plus-size representation in the fashion industry. Furthermore, in her job in marketing, working alongside creators, she constantly makes sure she hires queer creators, and not JUST in Pride season. Go Lottie!

"IT'S SO IMPORTANT TO TALK WHEN YOU'RE STRUGGLING, BECAUSE IT'S NOT ALWAYS STRAIGHTFORWARD"

ADAM ELI

Author Adam Eli has been an unstoppable activist in the queer community in the past few years and is someone I really look up to. He cofounded Voices 4, an NYC-based activist group that's focused on "queer liberation," and actively uses his social media to talk on a wide range of issues, including everything from dealing with homophobia or antisemitism to helping promote and organize rallies and protests during the pandemic. He speaks up for marginalized members of the queer community across the world and uses his voice to amplify theirs. Adam also combined all this activism work into a brilliant book, *The New Queer Conscience*.

When Gucci produced their first zine, *Chime For Change*, they turned to Adam to help edit it. Launching it with a huge campaign and full of queer talent, he helped mark a turning point in representation for LGBTQ+ creators in the fashion and print industries. He also frequently touches on body image within the queer community, reminding his audience that all bodies are beautiful. One of my favorite quotes was his tweet: "this is your permission to unfollow accounts that make you feel bad about your body."

"I LOVE BEING A QUEER JEW AND NOBODY CAN TAKE THAT AWAY FROM ME"

DEXTER MAYFIELD

Dexter Mayfield is a plus-size model, actor, and dancer who pushes for more visibility of plus-size queer people and body positivity within the queer community. He has walked and sashayed down a fashion catwalk for fashion designer Marco Marco, appeared in a J-Lo music video, and amassed a huge audience of fans that love him for his humor, fierce looks, and dance moves! I've never seen someone work a designer neon catsuit with matching neon high-heeled boots, but Dexter OWNS it.

He was the first ever queer Black plus-size man to walk a catwalk in LA Fashion Week, which further showed how much more representation is needed in the fashion industry for icons like Dexter. Since that show, his profile has continually grown, and he has become a prolific ambassador for men's body positivity. Speaking to *HuffPost* about seeing more plus-size models on billboards, he said, "I think that so many more young men will be confident in themselves and happy as the person they are if we can do that."

"I'M NOT GOING TO LET (MY BODY) BE AN EXCUSE FOR SOMEONE TO NOT TREAT ME WITH THE RESPECT, LOVE, AND CARE THAT I DESERVE"

SHIVA RAICHANDANI

A nonbinary artist and writer, Shiva Raichandani also writes and speaks about mental health, racism, LGBTQ+ politics, and the importance of more gender-diverse representation in the world. As the principal dancer and lead instructor for the London School of Bollywood, she helps lead a dance company that aims to use music and dance to challenge the ways in which gender-diverse people are represented universally and in Bollywood. So far the company has appeared and competed on *Britain's Got Talent* as well as the France and India versions of the series, with Shiva speaking about their routine on the latter: "With a routine like this in which a nonbinary gender fluid 'star' takes center stage instead of the quintessential 'hero' and 'heroine,' we hoped to add to the discourse around gender fluidity and queerness that is too often ignored in the Bollywood industry."

Shiva created and is also starting production on *Queer Parivaar*, a film set around an interfaith wedding of a queer couple that will cover themes such as the identities of nonbinary people, family bonds, and, of course, queer LOVE.

"I'LL STILL BE STRONG WITH THE LOVE I HAVE FOR MYSELF AND THE LOVE I HAVE TO OFFER"

JAMIE WINDUST

With bold lips, striking stars across their face, and a wardrobe I can only dream of pulling off, there is no one out there like Jamie. An author, writer, and contributing editor to *GAY TIMES*, Jamie identifies as nonbinary and frequently writes and shares their experiences navigating gender dysphoria and transphobia. Jamie openly talks about their mental health and how they deal with it day-to-day and has worked closely with many different charities and organizations.

As a nonbinary person, they face a lot of discrimination, and remind their huge audience of followers to be kind to themselves and to keep on fighting. With a huge focus on pushing to keep the Gender Recognition Act in the UK, Jamie has actively been working hard to raise awareness around the GRA and how it will benefit gender nonconforming and trans members of the LGBTQ+ community. They wrote: "Despite everything we portray, many of us are truly devastated and tired, but we WILL fight this." Jamie released their debut book, *In Their Shoes: Navigating Non-Binary Life*, in 2020, and it's an absolute must read.

"ALWAYS TRY AND REMEMBER THE JOY IN BEING US"

JILLIAN

Jillian Mercado is a disabled Latinx actress, activist, and model. Modeling for Diesel, Nordstrom, and Target AND appearing in magazines like *Teen Vogue* and *Cosmopolitan*, Jillian is pushing forward for even more representation of wheelchair-bound users and accessibility for them in the media, especially in the fashion industry. She often speaks about how people can be allies to the disabled community and what more they can do to make sure that authentic representation happens. Talking to *Teen Vogue*, she said, "If you have a position of power to actually be the one to change—or even if you're not—speak up about it."

Jillian is also the founder of Black Disabled Creatives, a platform to showcase a variety of different Black creatives with disabilities. This is a way for Jillian to create a safe space where she can, she says, help "bridge the divide for creatives with disabilities."

"IF YOU FEEL LIKE THE WORLD IS LETTING YOU DOWN, BE THE PERSON TO CHANGE IT"

HAYLEY
KIYOKO

Dubbed by her fans as "Lesbian Jesus," Hayley Kiyoko is a singer, writer, and actress. Her music centers on her own journey with her sexuality and her identity. She released the same-sex romance-themed video, "Girls Like Girls" in 2015, and aside from it being a certified tune, it has also garnered over 128 million views on YouTube. Like I said, it's a TUNE.

The music industry still has a long way to go in terms of queer representation, and being an openly queer singer like Hayley can take a toll on mental health. In 2019, she filmed a video for World Suicide Prevention Day and the "Seize the Awkward" campaign, talking about how she deals with her mental health on a regular basis and the stigma of being a queer singer. She discussed how she had reached a point where she couldn't *not* talk about it—"When you don't talk about it, you feel more isolated, you feel more alone, and I'm sure many of you go through those feelings . . . we *need* to talk about it."

CHERYL HOLE

Cheryl Hole is *THE* Essex Diva. One of the first contestants on the first ever series of *RuPaul's Drag Race UK*, Cheryl came, saw, conquered, and made a lasting impression on viewers. With her sparkling personality, self-deprecating humor and passion for pop-culture references, she became a firm fan favorite. However, she definitely dealt with some obstacles along the way. Earlier in the series she struggled with the pressure of being on a large televised platform, and that was affecting her own state of mind. She came through it though; in a beautiful moment of self-affirmation in her interview, wiping some tears away, she said, "I'm a f##king star." You ARE Cheryl!

Being thrust into the spotlight comes with its own fair share of people's negativity, and lots of fans reach out to her with their own problems. Being the babe she is, Cheryl always shares helpline numbers, words of advice, and important calls to action of how fans can seek support. Just one scroll at her Instagram and you'll find a whole lot of hair, sequins, stunning looks, and A LOT of heart.

"WHEN ALL ELSE FAILS, NEVER FORGET... YOU'RE A F##KING STAR!"

RIVER GALLO

I first came across River Gallo when I was told to watch a short film they had written, directed, and acted in called *Ponyboi*. Holy shit, I was not ready for the nineteen-minute emotional rollercoaster that the film took me on, but WOW. Watch it. Repeatedly. *Ponyboi* tells the story of an intersex runaway, played by River, who is looking for love and also trying to navigate their own intersex identity. It's game-changing, heart-breaking, and visually stunning. It also FINALLY has representation of an intersex character and actor on film, and truly touches on the topic of what their journey has been and what it is like for so many other intersex people out there.

River is nonbinary, queer, and a fantastic activist for intersex rights, repeatedly, openly talking about their own experiences, the importance of visibility for characters like Ponyboi, and ending nonconsensual surgery on intersex infants and youth. Icons like River need to have their stories told and their characters seen onscreen more, so make sure you watch *Ponyboi*, and then share how much you love it on social media. Furthermore, River is currently developing the short into a feature film. YES, RIVER! We'd love to see it!

Back in 2012, Frank Ocean, singer, songwriter, and rapper took to Tumblr (ugh, what a time!) and came out as queer in a powerful letter for the whole world to see. At the time, this was a huge step forward for representation of the LGBTQ+ community in the R&B and hip-hop industry.

In his letter, Frank opened up about his first true love and falling in love with another man when he was nineteen years old. This would be a huge turning point for many future queer musicians, with Lil Nas X citing Frank's coming out as having a lasting impact on him and how to be more open in his career.

Frank is a brilliantly talented songwriter and singer—his albums, *Channel Orange* and *Blonde*, have a mix of tracks that will make anyone cry and feel. Listening to them with his coming out in mind adds a new layer of vulnerability to his lyrics about queer loneliness, community, and healing. It's an impactful emotional symphony of sounds that I highly recommend numerous listens to.

"I FEEL LIKE A FREE MAN"

SMALL ACTS OF SELF-CARE FOR YOUR MENTAL HEALTH:

This is a list of things that genuinely work for me. If they don't work for you, do some googling and I'm sure you will find plenty other ideas out there, too. As queer people, we need to look after ourselves and sometimes just doing one of these a day is enough. Give yourself the time you deserve; you are a gift of a human being.

1. MAKE YOUR BED

You will feel like you've achieved something before your day has started. It's a game changer.

2. CREATE

Draw, paint, write a story. You don't even need to be good at it, just do it. Being creative helps you to express how you may be feeling in other ways if you feel you can't articulate it to someone.

3. TAKE A SOCIAL MEDIA BREAK

Having a few days off social media is a great way to re-center yourself and cut out any overwhelming feelings you've had. Only go back when YOU feel comfortable to.

4. MEET A FRIEND

Seeing a friend and openly talking about what is on your mind can really work. Just make sure it's the right friend, one that will listen, give you a hug, and eat ice cream with you nonstop all afternoon.

5. MAKE ALLOWANCES FOR YOURSELF

If you're having a good, bad, or "meh" day, that's okay. Don't make yourself feel bad about it.

6. LIGHT A CANDLE

I swear, a good candle can work and chill you out. Close your eyes for five minutes and do some . . .

7. BREATHING EXERCISES

Breathe in for four, hold for seven, and out for eight. This especially works for me when I'm very anxious.

8. RECOGNIZE HOW FAR YOU'VE COME

That bad day you had two weeks ago when you were upset and in bed? Two weeks later you've come through that. Remind yourself that whatever you're feeling at that time, you can face it. You can.

9. WERK OUT

I hate working out but a HIIT session or some yoga can really help me refocus on what I'm feeling and what I want to get out of that day.

10. GO FOR A WALK

Fresh air in your lungs is bliss and a walk is a great way to process your thinking.

11. READ A BOOK

Taking a few minutes away from a screen is great for your eyes, and hopefully by reading this right now you're feeling that benefit!

12. LISTEN TO CHER

Truthfully, magic always happens when you listen to Cher. Cher is a universal being that transcends time, space, and life. Her music will make you feel, dance, and shake your hips.

POWER!

It's Pride time! It's the one month of the year when we celebrate LGBTQ+ rights, push for change, and own our QUEER POWER. It's also when loads of brands put together Pride products to sell for one month only, but the less said about that the better . . . Pride is a time to remind ourselves of everyone that came before us to fight for the rights we have today. And to be aware of the other areas of the world where LGBTQ+ people are still discriminated against and the further work we need to do!

BILLY PORTER

Billy Porter is an actor, singer, and frequent server of jaw-droppingly fierce red-carpet looks. If you've watched *Pose*, you'll know him for his beautiful portrayal of Pray Tell, a role which saw him nominated for an Emmy. Billy's profile has continued to grow in the mainstream, along with the gloriously camp fashion moments he gives us, ranging from tuxedo ballgowns at the Oscars to an Egyptian god at the Met Gala and *that* fringed-hat moment. He uses these points in his life to redirect attention to the Black Lives Matter movement and LGBTQ+ rights across the world. In 2021, he shared his HIV status as positive.

Billy performed at the World Pride opening ceremony and London Pride in 2019. At the fully digital NYC Pride in 2020, he did a virtual performance and made sure to reaffirm and remind his audience that while there was no physical Pride, there was still a community out there for them: "Y'all #pride is a bit different this year, however, it's as important to embrace and support our community."

TAN FRANCE

Stylist and fashion expert Tan France is one of the first ever openly gay South Asian men to appear on a mainstream TV show, *Queer Eye*. Throughout the show he helps people empower themselves to be their best, most fabulous and authentic selves through fashion. Having the responsibility of his representation on such a large scale on a show like this, and gaining over three million followers on Instagram, is a big deal! And things just keep getting better for Tan—he has released a book and gone on to front his own fashion show for Netflix, *Next In Fashion*. This is the sort of representation the world needs more of!

Tan also frequently speaks about misconceptions within the LGBTQ+ community and what it's like to be openly gay and of color. Speaking to *Shortlist*, he addressed the privilege that comes with being white and gay, "where people are often white and see existing white people in their culture. They see themselves reflected, so they see a sense of acceptance. That's a kind of privilege people don't know they possess."

"WE MUST ALL BE ALIGNED IN THE MOVEMENT TOWARD EQUALITY FOR IT TO BE SUCCESSFUL"

LANDON CIDER

Landon Cider is the first drag king to ever compete in a televised drag competition, and, spoiler alert—he won! Appearing in season three of The Boulet Brothers' *Dragula* (check it out), Landon repeatedly delivered show-stopping looks to the show's key themes, Filth, Horror, and Glamour. He also spoke about the importance of representation for drag kings and nonbinary performers in the drag community. The community has a lot of talented performers who aren't cis men who struggle to get bookings and true visibility, so having Landon on *Dragula* competing alongside nonbinary performer Hollow Eve was fantastic to see, and in my personal opinion, so refreshing and important.

Historically, drag kings have been around since the 1900s, but they have been almost erased from queer history; Landon cites Stormé DeLarverie as one of their inspirations. As Landon has pointed out, he believes this is because a lot of people have the common misconception that drag kings are less entertaining than drag queens, but this view is rooted in misogyny. So next time you come across a drag performer on social media that isn't a cis man, follow them, support them, and share their art.

"I AM A PROUD CIS WOMAN, LESBIAN AND DRAG KING"

HUNTER SCHAFER

This wouldn't be a book about LGBTQ+ icons without a mention of a certain *Euphoria* cast member, would it? I can hear the theme tune kicking through my ears already! Hunter Schafer plays Jules Vaughn in the hit show, and just like her character, Hunter is also trans. Yes! Trans representation in television! *Euphoria* is her acting debut, and she is AMAZING as Jules. She's doesn't like to label her sexuality but has referred to herself as "bi or pan or something like that."

After being diagnosed with dysphoria in the ninth grade, Hunter began transitioning. With the internet having a growing trans community, she turned to sites like YouTube to help her further understand her gender and learning from other people's transition stories. She then went on to be a modeling sensation, serving looks for huge names like Versace, Prada, Vera Wang, and more. She's so fierce.

Hunter is also an LGBTQ+ rights activist, acting as a plaintiff in ACLU's 2016 lawsuit against North Carolina's anti-trans HB2 bill, also known as "the bathroom bill." While the bathroom bill was repealed, there are still numerous pieces of legislation that affect trans people across the United States, and Hunter continues to use her platforms to raise awareness about them. Writing for *i-D* magazine in 2017, she said, "We are on the forefront of a revolution in which identity and expression will take priority over the labels assigned to us at birth."

"THE DIFFERENT COLORS OF A RAINBOW IS THE DIFFERENT EXPERIENCES THAT CAN FALL UNDER ONE COMMUNITY"

AARON PHILIP

Signing with Elite Model Management at eighteen years old, Aaron Philip became the first Black transgender wheelchair user to do so. Since then she's been featured in numerous fashion publications, shows, AND even been interviewed by Naomi Campbell for *Paper* magazine. She is heavily focused on getting better visibility for disabled people and is on a mission to make sure this happens, so that disabled people everywhere know they're not alone and they're *seen*.

Aaron uses her social media to educate and involve her audience about the LGBTQ+ community. She reposts GoFundMe pages for those struggling financially, resource posts, and continually speaks about how people can be an ally. During the beginning of Pride week, she wrote: "Be more than an ally, learn to love, protect and understand Black trans people."

"LOVE BLACK TRANS PEOPLE AS MUCH AS YOU LOVE YOURSELF AND FIGHT FOR US THAT WAY"

SCHUYLER BAILAR

In 2015, Schuyler Bailar became the first openly transgender athlete to swim in NCAA Division I history. At the time, this was, and still is, a huge step forward for how trans athletes are viewed in sports. Originally, Schuyler swam for Harvard on the women's team but took a break for his mental health and to reassess. Eventually, his female coach on the women's team spoke to the coach of the men's team, as she wanted what was best for him, especially as he was transitioning at the time. The men's team took Schuyler on.

Since then Schuyler has gone on to be heavily involved in activism for the trans and LGBTQ+ community. He helped with the USA Swimming cultural inclusion guides for LGBTQ+ and Asian American Athletes. On Instagram, he is known for posing alongside a whiteboard on which he writes key messages around a number of current social and political issues. Each post differs, with subjects ranging from mental health to racism to trans rights. Posting about Pride season during the pandemic and Black Lives Matter protests in 2020, "he reminded his audience, "The first Pride was a police riot."

SHEA COULEÉ

If you've watched *RuPaul's Drag Race*, Shea Couleé will be a familiar name. A drag queen, musician, and activist, Shea has said it's important to her to use her career and platform to inspire people, especially Black women and drag performers: "My Drag in its purest form is a love letter to Black women." She serves looks that always have a narrative and message linked to them for her audience to pick up on and learn from.

A firm fan favorite with a loyal following, Shea also utilizes her community to engage in her activism work and speak up against racism. The same month as Pride 2020, she was spotted at the Drag March for Change in support of Black Lives Matter. Someone recorded a video of her, out of drag, taking to the stage to speak to a crowd of protesters: "We need to make space. If y'all want to see it for us, pull up and open your purse. My name is Shea Couleé and I didn't come to play; I came to dismantle white supremacy."

"IT IS MY DUTY AS A BLACK PERSON, AND AS A BLACK PERSON WITH A PLATFORM, TO SPEAK OUT ABOUT THIS"

TRAVIS ALABANZA

A lot of people in this book are multitalented—and Travis Alabanza is no exception! Identifying as trans-feminine and gender nonconforming, Travis is a writer, actor, performer, and theater maker. Growing up as Black and queer in Bristol, England, they would use art to help them navigate and deal with the ignorance they were facing at the time. Cut to the present day, and they are one of the most prolific creatives on the queer scene, performing solo plays, speaking at (over forty) universities, and consistently using their online platform to speak up for change for the trans and gender nonconforming communities.

During Pride season, trans and nonbinary people don't always get the chance to take up the space their cis white queer counterparts do. Speaking to *GAY TIMES*, Travis mentioned how the gay community still has work to do to help the trans community, especially around Pride season: ". . . care about how we're getting home from the party. I think for me that is the focal point: to see us outside of just being fierce and to see us also as just people."

"INTERSECTIONALITY IS REAL, FINDING SOMEWHERE TO BELONG IS BEAUTIFUL & I LOVE BEING A GAY MAN"

MNEK is a Grammy-nominated chart-topping singer and songwriter. You most likely have heard one of his hits, whether it's sung by him or written by him. He has worked with a long list of huge musical talents including Beyoncé, Little Mix, Dua Lipa, Christina Aguilera, and Madonna, to name just a FEW (the list is endless). In 2018, he released his first solo album entitled *Language* and headlined UK Black Pride that same year. I can safely say that album is full of certified bops, including "Tongue," the lead single, the video for which featured MNEK vogueing in a hot pink matching shirt and trousers combo that, to be honest, is an iconic moment.

Aside from headlining at various queer events, he is a huge advocate for the queer community and also pushes for more representation in the music industry for Black and PoC queer people. Teaming up with Pride in Music in 2019, MNEK hosted a writing camp for LGBTQ+ songwriters for them to write, create, and produce with a number of other queer performers, to help them gain further opportunities in music.

"AS LONG AS MY PEOPLE DON'T HAVE THEIR RIGHTS ALL ACROSS AMERICA, THERE'S NO REASON FOR CELEBRATION"

Marsha P. Johnson's legacy will never be forgotten. An African American transgender activist and trailblazer, she was a prominent figure in the origins of Pride and did a lot of work for the queer rights movement in the 1960s and 70s. She said the "P" stood for "Pay it no mind," a phrase she would use when someone had something transphobic to say about her appearance. A sex worker and drag performer, Marsha was an essential part of the New York City gay scene in Greenwich Village and also during the Stonewall riots and the protests that followed. She was passionate about social justice and getting equal rights for everyone, especially the trans and Black trans community. She was known for her infectious smile, warm personality, and visual aesthetic of bright wigs, flowers, and limitless kindness and generosity.

During the Stonewall riots, Marsha P. Johnson and a number of other queer people resisted arrest. This led to a series of protests and riots, and a month later, the first organized queer rights march took place in New York City. In 1992, Marsha went missing and her body was found six days later. To this day the Black trans community are still extremely vulnerable. Over fifty-seven trans or gender nonconforming people were killed in the United States in 2021, the majority of which were Black and Latinx trans women.

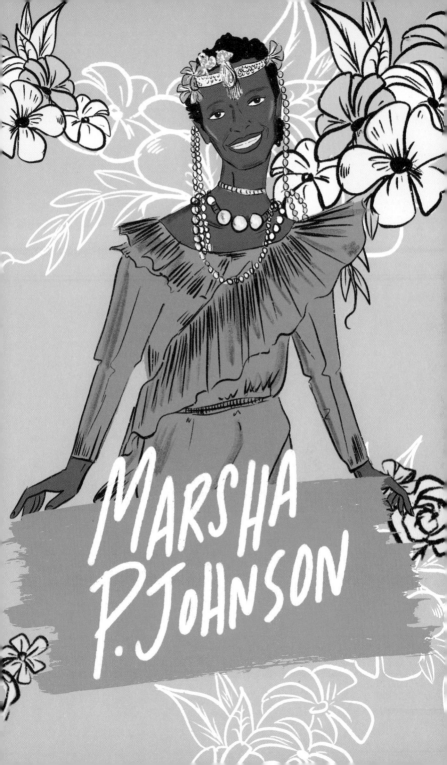

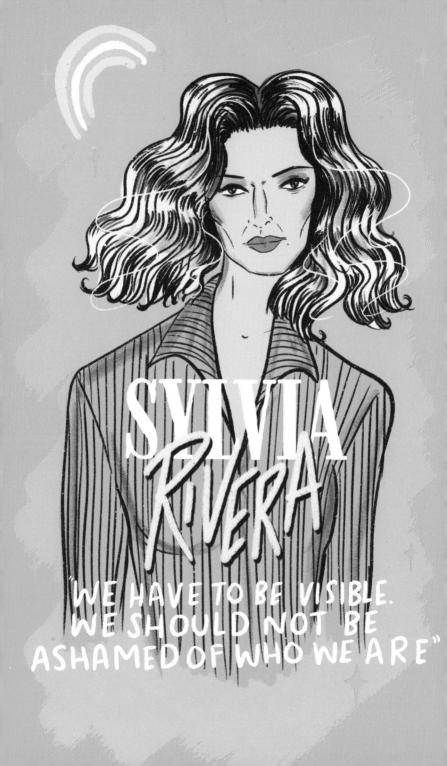

Another crucial person in the origins of Pride, Sylvia Rivera was a Latina American transgender rights activist who was at the forefront of the gay rights movement and the fight for equality. A community worker in New York, Sylvia also cofounded the Street Transvestite Action Revolutionaries (STAR) alongside her good friend Marsha P. Johnson. The group was set up to help homeless members of the LGBTQ+ community, including trans women, drag queens, and others and led to Sylvia and Marsha fighting for the Sexual Orientation Non-Discrimination Act in New York.

Sylvia passionately fought for trans rights, as, at the time, trans people weren't even fully accepted by the gay community or the gay rights movement. She took to the stage at the Christopher Street Liberation Day Rally in 1973 and even though she was met with boos from the crowd, she persisted, grabbing the mic and addressing them: "If it wasn't for the drag queen, there would be no gay liberation movement. We're the front liners!" Having passed away in 2014, Sylvia is still remembered today. In 2021, a monument of Marsha P. Johnson and Sylvia Rivera was built in Greenwich Village, just a few blocks away from the Stonewall Inn to honor their legacy.

STORMÉ DE LARVERIE

Stormé DeLarverie was an entertainer, activist, and a drag king who often performed as part of the Jewel Box Revue, which in 1955 was the United States' first racially integrated drag cabaret, which toured around the country. At that time there weren't many drag kings around, never mind performing, and, even over fifty years later, they are still underrepresented (as Landon Cider pointed out earlier). Then not in her drag persona, Stormé was known offstage for her gender nonconforming appearance, embracing her androgyny and often styling herself in men's suits and hats. This led to her being photographed by the influential and iconic Diane Arbus.

Working as a bouncer and volunteer street worker, Stormé was seen as a fierce protector of the lesbian community in New York City. During the Stonewall uprising, many butch lesbians were there that night and many believe she was the person who encouraged the crowd to fight back against the police, with eyewitnesses saying a woman fitting her appearance resisted arrest numerous times, was handcuffed, and hit over the head by a policeman with a baton. She turned to the crowd watching and allegedly said, "Why don't you guys do something?" As she was loaded into the back of a police vehicle, the crowd began to stir and rise up against what was happening. For the fiftieth anniversary of the Stonewall riots in 2019, the Stonewall National Monument was unveiled, which honored fifty American prominent figures as part of the National LGBTQ Wall Of Honor (this sits within the SNM). Stormé was one of them.

"IT WAS A REBELLION, IT WAS AN UPRISING, IT WAS A CIVIL RIGHTS DISOBEDIENCE—IT WASN'T NO DAMN RIOT"

> "**NO** TO RACISM.
> TO HOMOPHOBIA
> TO BIPHOBIA.
> TO TRANSPHOBIA
> TO ISLAMOPHOBIA.
> **PUT YOUR FISTS UP IN SOLIDARITY!**"

There are not enough words to describe my love and adoration for Phyll Opoku-Gyimah, aka Lady Phyll. She is the cofounder, trustee, and executive director of UK Black Pride—the UK's biggest LGBTQ+ event and safe space for queer Black people and queer people of color.

I went to my first UK Black Pride only a few years ago. It was THE most important Pride event I have been to. It promoted inclusivity, equality, and anti-racism. Lady Phyll takes to the stage and her words galvanize and stir a crowd, reminding a whole intersectional part of our queer community how important they are and how their voices need to be raised.

In 2016, Phyll turned down the opportunity to receive the MBE in the New Year Honours List. She told *DIVA* magazine, "As a trade unionist, a working-class girl and an out Black African lesbian, I want to stand to my principles and values." And that she DID.

Lady Phyll has continued to speak up and encourages others to do so. At the 2019 World Pride celebrations in New York City, she was invited on to the main stage where she took to the mic, fist held high in the air, to say, "No to racism. No to homophobia. No to biphobia. No to transphobia. No to islamophobia. Put your fists up in solidarity!"

Icon. Queen. Trailblazer. Thank you, Lady Phyll, for everything you do.

WAYS TO CELEBRATE PRIDE SEASON ALL YEAR ROUND:

Pride is ALL THE TIME, baby. Here are some ways to find queerness in everyday life and celebrate yourself and your community with loved ones.

1. READ, LISTEN, AND WATCH

Every year there is new LGBTQ+ content released. This means you can stream queer shows, listen to queer music, and read queer books. Immerse yourself in the culture and community. You'll be educated, inspired, and proud.

2. SUPPORT QUEER FUNDS AND CHARITIES

There are numerous queer funds and charities that need your support. Instead of spending a tenner on a rainbow fan, consider donating that money to a charity. If you can't financially support, share the charity's page on your socials and let your friends know. I think it's important to give back to the community, especially supporting charities or funds centered around Black or PoC queer people. As a white queer, I'm aware of my privilege and what I can do to help those marginalized in our community.

3. GO TO LGBTQ+ STUFF

You can attend a number of events, art shows, plays, museum exhibitions, and more throughout the year that have LGBTQ+ themes. These are great ways to celebrate Pride and also support the talent involved!

4. REACH OUT

There are times where we will need a friend or a family member. Do not hesitate to reach out to somebody who can listen and love you. Being queer is an experience that is unique to each of us and at times we can be triggered and need to talk. There is also nothing wrong with using a helpline with a qualified volunteer on the other end. Don't be alone in your feelings.

5. THROW AN EVENT

There's nothing stopping you having family, chosen family, and friends over for a night of proud anthems. A glitter curtain will change your life FOREVER. Get some cocktails going, put some tunes on, steal Auntie Carol's disco leggings from the 80s, and have your very own queer safe space party!

6. DRESS TO IMPRESS

I love to serve a lewk on the way to the bus stop, and there's nothing stopping you either! Not all queer people are queer "presenting"; however, if you want to dress that way, do it. You can celebrate your rainbowtasticness and identity through experimenting with fashion, styling, and makeup. And don't forget to own the street like a catwalk when you do. WERK!

7. SHARE ON YOUR SOCIAL

Use your social media to share LGBTQ+-related content to help your followers understand we're still fighting for LGBTQ+ rights across the world.

8. BUY A GLITTER CURTAIN

If you didn't get the hint before, you really need to, hun. They will take your space from cute kitchen to DISCO ELEGANZA.

OUTRO

There isn't one way to be "queer." Personally, I found this out at an early age when I genuinely thought all gay men were meant to act like Jack in *Will & Grace*. While some do, I could NOT pull off that look. Don't forget what makes up the brilliant DNA of YOU. Queer people come in all shapes, sizes, personalities, and fabulousness, and however you feel you *should* be, don't—just BE. For the record, this book and myself totally accept you, and I'm sending you a big invisible hug right now. You got this. And while you've read this book on queer icons and their stories, take a minute to think of your story, your life, and what you've navigated to be here—you're an icon yourself and you have that queer power inside of you. Always.

THANK YOU!

This book is dedicated to my friends Anick Soni, Blair Imani, Tess Holliday, Freida Slaves, Julian Gavino, Alexander Leon, Arun Blair-Mangat, Kenny Ethan Jones, Juno Dawson, Radam Ridwan, Charlie Craggs, Crystal Rasmussen, Sabah Choudrey, Jade Thirlwall, TeTe Bang, Tanya Compass, Cheddar Gorgeous, Jessie Ware, Char Ellesse, Lottie L'Amour, Adam Eli, Shiva Raichandani, Jamie Windust, Cheryl Hole, River Gallo, Cheryl, Travis Alabanza, MNEK, Lady Phyll . . . and my mum, Madeleine.

I also want to take a minute to thank all the icons who were involved in this book and have supported it. It's truly been a dream of mine to create a book that amplifies voices in the LGBTQ+ community that need to be heard more, so THANK YOU for being part of this journey! Rainbows and cuddles to all of you. Massive cuddles and thanks go to the incredible team at Penguin Workshop who have worked so hard to bring Queer Power to the US audience! With new icons and extra text, there was a fair amount of extra work, and I'm so thankful to Rachel Sonis, Julia Rosenfeld, and Shara Hardeson for making it as smooth as possible. You're all awesome. What a team! Big Thank You to Lauren Gardner, aka The LG, for continually being a great agent, someone who has my best interests at heart, listens and is still my own little personal rainbow. I'm very lucky to have an LG, AND to Justine Smith who helped with the US development and editing. Lastly, a big thanks to all my family and friends who have supported me throughout this process and been total babes. I love you all! And finally, thank YOU to whoever is reading this. Thank you for supporting this book, these voices, and these messages. Take them with you into the world and share the love.

WAYS TO SUPPORT

On these pages are just *some* of the different organizations and funds you can support!

THE MARSHA P. JOHNSON INSTITUTE—a nonprofit organization protecting the rights of Black transgender people. https://marshap.org/

GLSEN—a national nonprofit organization working to improve support for LGBTQ+ youth in schools. https://www.glsen.org/

TRANS WEEK—a platform and campaign to fight anti-trans legislation and elevate trans joy, liberation, and power. https://www.trans-week.com/

THE TREVOR PROJECT—the world's largest suicide prevention and crisis intervention organization for LGBTQ+ people. https://www.thetrevorproject.org/

GLAAD—a nongovernmental organization working through entertainment and media to share stories from the LGBTQ+ community. https://www.glaad.org/

SYLIVIA RIVERA LAW PROJECT—an organization that helps improve access to social, health, and legal services for transgender people who are low-income, people of color, and immigrants. https://srlp.org/

STONEWALL COMMUNITY FOUNDATION—a community foundation for lesbian, gay, bisexual, transgender, queer, and ally donors, volunteers, and grant and scholarship seekers. https://www.stonewallfoundation.org/

COLOURS YOUTH NETWORK—supports young people of color to explore and celebrate who they are through events, workshops, and more. http://www.coloursyouthnetwork.com/

TRANS LIFELINE—a nonprofit organization that offers emotional and financial support to trans people in crisis. https://translifeline.org/

FOR THE GWORLS—a Black, trans-led collective that curates parties to fundraise money to help support Black transgender people with gender-affirming surgeries, travel, rent, and more. https://www.forthegworls.party/home

PRIDE FOUNDATION—an LGBT philanthropic foundation building a "better, safer, and more equitable world for LGBTQ+ people." https://pridefoundation.org/

GENDERED INTELLIGENCE—a trans-led charity working across the United Kingdom to increase understandings of gender diversity. https://genderedintelligence.co.uk/

EXIST LOUDLY FUND—an organization for queer Black youth to find a community and a chosen family, and to explore their identity through digital and online workshops. Instagram: @existloudly

UK BLACK PRIDE—is "Europe's largest celebration for LGBTQI+ people of African, Asian, Caribbean, Latin American, and Middle Eastern" heritage. https://www.ukblackpride.org.uk/

IMAAN—the leading LGBTQ+ Muslim organization in the United Kingdom. https://imaanlondon.wordpress.com/

THEY/THEM COLLECTIVE—a mutual aid collective that supports "queer, non-binary, trans, Black, brown, and Indigenous liberation." Instagram: @theythemcollective

HELPLINES

If you need to reach out and just have a talk, you can always call these numbers, text, or do live chat with these links.

THE TREVOR PROJECT—866-488-7386
https://www.thetrevorproject.org/get-help/

988 SUICIDE AND CRISIS LIFELINE—Call or text: 988
Or call: 800-273-TALK (800-273-8255)
Spanish: 888-628-9454
https://988lifeline.org/talk-to-someone-now/

TRANS LIFELINE—877-565-8860

CRISIS TEXT LINE—Text START to 741-741

LGBT NATIONAL YOUTH TALKLINE—800-246-7743

THE NATIONAL RUNAWAY SAFELINE—800-RUNAWAY
(800-786-2929)
https://www.1800runaway.org/

NATIONAL AIDS HOTLINE—800-448-0440

RESOURCES

STREAM IT!

LANGUAGE By MNEK (album)

SAWAYAMA
By Rina Sawayama (album)

"LOVE YOURSELF"
By Billy Porter (song)

PALO SANTO
By Years & Years (album)

CONFETTI By Little Mix (album)

"FIGHT FOR THIS LOVE"
By Cheryl (song)

CLARITY By Kim Petras (album)

CHROMATICA
By Lady Gaga (album)

WHAT'S YOUR PLEASURE?
By Jessie Ware (album)

111 By Pabllo Vittar (album)

BETWEEN US By Little Mix (album)

MONTERO By Lil Nas X (album)

CHANNEL ORANGE By Frank Ocean (album)

BLONDE By Frank Ocean (album)

CHEAP QUEEN By King Princess (album)

DIRTY COMPUTER
By Janelle Monáe (album)

RESOURCES

WATCH IT!

THE INTERSEX DIARIES
(documentary, BBC Radio 1 Stories)
POSE (drama series, FX)
PARIS IS BURNING
(documentary film, 1990)
SEX EDUCATION
(comedy-drama series, Netflix)
QUEER EYE (reality show, Netflix)
RUPAUL'S DRAG RACE (reality
show, Logo TV/VH1)
THE BOULET BROTHERS'
DRAGULA (reality show,
Netflix/Amazon Prime)
PRIDE (feature film, 2014)
DISCLOSURE
(documentary, Netflix)
LEGENDARY (reality show, HBO)
PAY IT NO MIND – THE LIFE
AND TIMES OF MARSHA P.
JOHNSON (documentary, 2012)
A FANTASTIC WOMAN
(feature film, 2017)
PONYBOI (feature film, 2019)
SPECIAL (comedy series, Netflix)
IT'S A SIN (limited series,
HBO MAX)
QUEER PARIVAAR (short film,
2022)

RESOURCES

READ IT!

MAKING OUR WAY HOME: THE GREAT MIGRATION AND THE BLACK AMERICAN DREAM By Blair Imani (Ten Speed Press, 2020)

THE GENDER GAMES: THE PROBLEM WITH MEN AND WOMEN, FROM SOMEONE WHO HAS BEEN BOTH By Juno Dawson (Two Roads, 2017)

THE NEW QUEER CONSCIENCE By Adam Eli (Penguin Workshop, 2020)

BEYOND THE GENDER BINARY By Alok Vaid-Menon (Penguin Workshop, 2020)

YOUR WOUND / MY GARDEN By Alok Vaid-Menon (Self published, 2021)

THE BLACK FLAMINGO By Dean Atta (Hodder, 2019)

NATURALLY TAN: A MEMOIR By Tan France (Virgin Books, 2019)

THE TRANSSEXUAL FROM TOBAGO By Dominique Jackson (CreateSpace, 2014)

LOCKDOWN LOOKBOOK By Radam Ridwan (2020)

TO MY TRANS SISTERS Edited by Charlie Craggs (Jessica Kingsley, 2017)

OVER THE TOP: MY STORY By Jonathan Van Ness (Simon & Schuster, 2019)

IN THEIR SHOES: NAVIGATING NON-BINARY LIFE By Jamie Windust (Jessica Kingsley Publishers, 2020)

FREE TO BE ME: AN LGBTQ+ JOURNAL OF LOVE, PRIDE & FINDING YOUR INNER RAINBOW By Dom&Ink (Penguin Workshop, 2019)

CONTINUUM By Chella Man (Penguin Workshop, 2021)

SUPPORTING TRANS PEOPLE OF COLOUR By Sabah Choudrey (Jessica Kingsley Publishers, 2021)

RESOURCES

LISTEN TO IT!

QMMUNITY (podcast)
ANTHEMS (podcast)
A GAY AND A NONGAY (podcast)
MAKING GAY HISTORY (podcast)
QUEER AF (podcast)
GETTING CURIOUS WITH
JONATHAN VAN NESS (podcast)
LGBTQ&A (podcast)

SOURCES

p13 *The Intersex Diaries*, BBC Radio 1 Stories, 2018; p16 "I'm Coming Out," NikkieTutorials, YouTube, 2020; p21 *Nylon*, 2019; p23 "Partly why Freida is still Freida is so . . . You see a Black drag queen, just living her best life": "A Celebration of London's Diverse, Queer Drag Culture" by Jess Kohl; p31 *NME*, March 2020; p32 "It allows me to embrace my otherness; it celebrates that": *Attitude*, January 2020; p35 *Vulture*, April 2019; p42 TomboyX, 2018; p50 "The big problem for non-binary people like me isn't just being seen – it's being seen as human": *PinkNews*, July 2020; p53 *ELLE* magazine, May 2019; p58 *NPR Fresh Air*, August 2019; p69 *GAY TIMES* Amplify, July 2020; p70 Dwyane Wade on *The Ellen Show*, February 2020; p73 *Attitude*, May 2020; p74 *Attitude*, April 2019; p76 Stonewall rally, June 2019; p78 *Vogue*, June 27, 2020; p80 *GAY TIMES,* 2019; p85 *Dazed Digital*, November 2019; p87 *GAY TIMES*, 2019; p88 *GAY TIMES*, June 2020; p95 *New York Times*, October 2019; p103 *Attitude*, July 2020; p108 *GAY TIMES*, 2019; p111 *Billboard*, March 2018; p114 *Subvrt*, June 2020; p123 *Evening Standard*, July 2019; p124 *Image*, June 10, 2020; p127 *GAY TIMES*, 2019; p128 *i-D* magazine, March 2017; p132 *The Grace Gazette*, October 2019; p135 *Esquire*, June 2020; p136 *Metro*, October 2019.